LSAT®
ESSAY WRITING
STRATEGIES AND TACTICS

SECOND EDITION

BOB VERINI

This publication is designed to provide accurate and authoritative information in regard to the subject matter covered. It is sold with the understanding that the publisher is not engaged in rendering legal, accounting, or other professional service. If legal advice or other expert assistance is required, the services of a competent professional should be sought.

© 2013 Kaplan, Inc.

Published by Kaplan Publishing, a division of Kaplan, Inc.
395 Hudson Street
New York, NY 10014

Printed in the United States of America

10 9 8 7 6 5 4 3

ISBN: 978-1-61865-311-6

Kaplan Publishing books are available at special quantity discounts to use for sales promotions, employee premiums, or educational purposes. For more information or to purchase books, please call the Simon & Schuster special sales department at 866-506-1949.

Table of Contents

About the Experts

Veteran Kaplan teacher and curriculum designer **BOB VERINI** has played a significant role in the design and development of Kaplan's LSAT and other programs for over 30 years. Having taken standardized tests multiple times and to multiple perfect scores, he has turned his first-hand expertise into lessons and question explanations used in live classes, recordings, and retail books (including this one), that arguably have impacted more students' careers in the past quarter century than the work of any other individual. Bob currently serves as the Director of Academic Quality for Kaplan's Digital Media Group, while continuing to enhance applicants' admission chances as an online LSAT teacher and law school admissions consultant.

Kaplan is the #1 Choice for LSAT Prep! With more than 70 years of experience, Kaplan's products and programs are designed with students in mind. Our unique combination of the highest quality study materials, realistic testing experience, and dynamic tutors is unrivaled. We provide the most personalized prep with more options than any competitor—including classroom courses, online programs, small group and one-on-one tutoring, and self-study guides. In fact, Kaplan's prep is so focused and effective, Kaplan guarantees students' scores will improve—or they receive their money back.

How to Use This Booklet

Congratulations! You're well on your way to mastering the LSAT, with your purchase of Kaplan's complete three-book set of *LSAT Logic Games: Strategies and Tactics*, *LSAT Logical Reasoning: Strategies and Tactics*, and *LSAT Reading Comprehension: Strategies and Tactics*.

In this supplemental booklet, you'll find tips and strategies you can use to master the Writing Sample section of the LSAT, from an expert Kaplan instructor. Kaplan has the resources to help you be prepared for anything you encounter on test day, and to help you maximize your LSAT score.

For more information on Kaplan's LSAT products and programs, please visit us at www.kaptest.com/LSAT.

Good luck!

ABOUT THE LSAT

The LSAT is a standardized test written by the Law School Admission Council (LSAC) and administered four times each year. The test is a required component of your application to all American Bar Association–approved law schools as well as some others.

The LSAT is designed to measure the skills necessary for success in your first year of law school (according to the governing bodies of law schools), such as strategic reading, analyzing arguments, understanding formal logic, and making deductions. Because these skills will serve you well throughout law school and your professional life, consider your LSAT preparation an investment in your career.

You may already possess some level of proficiency with LSAT-tested skills. However, you probably haven't yet mastered how to use those skills to your best advantage in the context of a standardized, skills-based test that requires careful time management.

The LSAT is also a test of endurance—five 35-minute blocks of multiple-choice testing plus a 35-minute writing sample. Add in the administrative tasks at both ends of the test and a 10- to 15-minute break midway through, and you can count on being in the test room for at least four and a half hours. It's a grueling experience, but it's not as bad if you are familiar with the test and ready to handle every section. You want to approach the test with confidence so that you can maintain your focus, limit your stress, and get your highest score on test day. That's why it's so important to take control of the test, just as you will take control of the rest of the application process.

Our material is as up-to-date as possible at the time of this printing, but test specifications may change at any time. Please visit our website at http://kaptest.com/LSAT for the latest news and updates.

How Do I Register for the LSAT?

The LSAT is administered by the Law School Admission Council (LSAC). Be sure to register as soon as possible, as your preferred test site can fill up quickly. You can register for the LSAT in three ways:

- Online: Sign up at http://lsac.org.
- Telephone: Call LSAC at (215) 968-1001.
- Email: Contact LSAC for a registration packet at lsacinfo@lsac.org.

If you have additional questions about registration, contact the LSAC by phone or by email.

ABOUT THE WRITING SAMPLE

On the LSAT, you will be given a prompt consisting of a problem, two criteria or goals that must be met in addressing the problem, and two possible courses of action. You'll have 35 minutes at the end of your LSAT day to make a written case for your position.

Your essay must be confined to the space provided, which is roughly the equivalent of two sheets of standard lined paper. Note that there's really no time or space to change your mind or radically alter your essay once you've begun writing, so *plan your argument carefully before beginning to write*. Make sure to write as legibly as you can.

The Writing Sample is ungraded, but it is sent to law schools along with your LSAT score. In fact, it's the second page admissions committee members see when they open and review your packet. Many law schools use the Writing Sample to help make decisions on borderline cases or to decide between applicants with otherwise comparable credentials. Granted, it may not carry the same weight as the scored sections of the test, but because it can have an impact on your admission chances, your best bet is to take it seriously.

LSAT Writing Sample Strategies and Tactics

by Bob Verini

DO LAW SCHOOLS ACTUALLY READ THE LSAT WRITING SAMPLE?

Yes, of course they do.

Actually, "My goodness, yes, of course" was the response of a law school admissions director from a prestigious East Coast institution. She seemed surprised I would even ask whether LSAC and its members would go to all the trouble and expense of creating, writing, administering, and distributing a writing exercise in which none of them was interested. (Much less do so for the better part of the last 30 years.)

But there may be cynics, and I'll start by addressing them first. **Yes, they read it,** and those who read it take it seriously.

Now, not everyone reads it with the same interest, at the same point in the application review process, or with the same purpose in mind. But saying that some law schools give the Writing Sample a quick look, while others invest it with importance, is very different from the cavalier assumption that as an unscored portion of your LSAT, the Writing Sample is superfluous and deserves no attention.

In this section I will tell you exactly what law schools are looking for, why the Writing Sample serves their purposes, and how to approach the exercise as practically and systematically as these books have (I hope) persuaded you to approach the scored LSAT.

WHAT ARE LAW SCHOOLS LOOKING TO GAUGE, AND WHY?

Three things, but remember, it's mysterious as to which law schools value which of the three. (Some value them all.) If you hit all the bases, you'll have nothing to fear. They want to assess:

Your relationship with the English language. The commerce of the law student is the written word. You will churn out a ton of writing over three years. As such it behooves the admissions committee to judge: Are you and the language on buddy-buddy terms, or are you acquaintances, or have you barely even met? The more easy and fluent your writing under tightly timed, reference-book-free circumstances, the more likely it is that the predominant mode of your law school training won't be a strain for you.

admissions
TIP

Highlight debate
background in your
application if you have
any. It's an excellent
"DNA marker" for
law school success.

admissions
TIP

Make sure your personal
statement doesn't
sound so polished as
to raise doubts. As the
substitute for a personal
face-to-face interview
it's supposed to sound
like you anyway, so that
shouldn't be a problem.

Your affinity for argument. The law is a process whereby two sides attempt to persuade an audience of their reasoning while weakening the arguments on the other side. Alas, the days in which all college students, law school bound or not, were trained in rhetoric and debate are behind us. Because most applicants haven't engaged in formal debate, law schools like to see that you have a sense of how to create a persuasively phrased conclusion, know how to support it with appropriate evidence, and are able to make reasonable assumptions in connecting the two.

The degree of help you received in your Personal Statement. Here's another quote from an admissions professional: "We understand that applicants have experts look over the personal statement to proofread and make edits, but we like to know that it's the applicant's own work. And while we don't expect the LSAT essay to be at all polished, it does provide a basis for comparison as to the applicant's writing ability." I take this as code for: "If the word choice, syntax, punctuation and structure are markedly different in the off the cuff writing vs. the personal statement, we might smell a rat."

OKAY, I'M PERSUADED.
SO HOW EXACTLY IS THE EXERCISE STRUCTURED?

The structure of the **prompt** is always the same. A **Decision Maker** (or "D-M"—an individual, married couple, organization, municipality, or other institution) is choosing between two distinct alternatives. Two of the D-M's bulleted **Criteria** are listed. As a rule, one criterion will tend to favor the first alternative or option; the other, the second. Both **Options** have pros and cons in terms of the criteria; neither is a slam dunk.

Your job is to *argue for one of them over the other*—which means you have to come up with as solid an argument as you can for **"The Winner"** (which is what we'll call the one you favor), while attempting to shoot down the appeal of the one you choose as **"The Loser."**

As you'll see, the predetermined prompt structure means that you can pretty much predetermine your Writing Sample structure as well.

WHAT IS MY ROLE OR PERSONA IN ALL OF THIS?

Think of yourself as an outside consultant, one with no personal stake in the outcome. You don't care which nursing home Mrs. Jones goes to, or which location Mr. and Mrs. Smith pick for their new restaurant. You're given criteria and facts, and based on your assumptions as to how the world works, you take a stand and support it. If Jones or the Smiths don't like your choice or reasoning, they're free to reject it. And you'll shrug that off, because you were asked for your opinion and gave it.

TIP

Don't be any more enthusiastic about the choice than your reading of the criteria and your assumptions allow you to be. If you're 100% sure, fine; if you're lukewarm, that's fine too. Just keep the tone of your writing in sync with your feelings.

Some writers (including me) have written an occasional Writing Sample in which the essential point was, "Both of these alternatives sound fundamentally flawed, and if I were the Smiths I'd keep looking." It's a bold choice, and could be the topic for the final paragraph of your Writing Sample if you truly do believe the alternatives are horrible. Still and all, you have to follow instructions: You have to hold your nose and say in effect, "With a gun to my back I guess I'd tell the Smiths to choose Option X, for these reasons."

APPROACHING THE PROMPT: BRAINSTORMING AND PLANNING

First things first: Make sure you have a handle on the overall situation, being sure to accurately paraphrase the key elements. Pore through this prompt from 2007:

A neighborhood association is planning to sponsor a public event on the first day of summer—either a walking tour or a 5 kilometer run. Using the facts below, write an essay in which you argue for one event over the other based on the following two criteria:

- The association wants to encourage more neighborhood residents to become association members.
- In order to conduct other activities during the year, the association wants to minimize the time and resources required by the event.

The first event is a free, self-guided walking tour of some of the neighborhood's private homes and historic buildings. The tour would feature the association's promotional table and exhibits of crafts, music, and cooking. Many neighborhood residents have expressed interest in such a tour. Some of the responsibility for organizing the event would be borne by those who own the homes and buildings; the association would be responsible for the remaining details. The costs of this event would consume most of the association's annual budget. Other neighborhood associations that have conducted similar tours report robust neighborhood participation and accompanying increases in membership.

The second event is a 5 kilometer run through the neighborhood. The association has sponsored this yearly event for almost a decade. In recent years, the association has hired a third-party company to manage the race and would do so again. Registration fees collected from race participants would cover administrative costs. In the past the event has led to modest increases in membership for the association. At its peak, almost 1,000 people participated in the race, most of them from out of town. This year more people are expected to participate because the course has been professionally certified and the race would serve as a qualifying race for a national championship.*

Your **D-M**, the association, will (you hope) sponsor whichever event you choose, "the tour" or "the race." (You don't need to refer to the options any other way.)

Have you read through the two **Options**? Hope so, but don't jump to a conclusion! As a good consultant you want to weigh everything—within time limits—before taking a stand. Reserve judgment until you go through these steps, starting with a serious perusal of the two Criteria.

---

* PrepTest 52, Writing Sample Topic

BRAINSTORMING STEP #1:
Think through and paraphrase the Criteria.

Starting with bullet point #1: How would a neighborhood group encourage new members? Should they emphasize the camaraderie and friendship? Ought they play up the elements of fun? Will they get better results by organizing adult activities or appealing to the entire family? How do you turn nonjoiners into joiners?

Here's where your own personal experiences and assumptions can and should come into play. Whatever you know, or have learned, or believe about people's behavior is fodder for your essay, because all of that is what fundamentally guides your judgment. Here's what one student jotted down:

> <u>Goal</u>: Build members: Emphasize advantages of joining. Make it seem like fun not work,
> make the value of joining clear. Appeal to civic pride / property values. Shld be family oriented.

It doesn't matter whether you agree or disagree, but whether you bring some independent thought to the process. Here's how that same student assessed the second criterion:

> <u>Goal</u>: Minimize time/resources: Keep it cheap. Shldn't need to learn new procedures/logistics.
> As few organizers as possible, pref. unpaid volunteers. Organize fast, and not far in advance.

If phrases other than these came to you, that's great. Notice that the student shows no awareness of having read the descriptions of the tour and the run. That's good! She has endeavored to take the criteria on face value first.

Now you have a deeper understanding of what the D-M wants. You've also come up with some ideas, and even some phrases, likely to end up in your essay.

BRAINSTORMING STEP #2:
Decide whether unmentioned criteria—if any—are, in your judgment, also relevant to consider beyond the ones provided.

You don't *have* to come up with additional factors worth considering, but if you do and can justify your reasoning, why not? Our student made this note on her scratch paper:

> *Raising $ is always good for an organization.*

In other words, even though the bullet points don't explicitly reference money, it may make sense to factor in how much cash will be required *and* how much cash, if any, an activity is likely to bring in. Just food for thought.

TIP

You can't substitute your own new criterion for the ones offered, but you are certainly permitted to supplement your argument with it.

BRAINSTORMING STEP #3:

Think through how you'd argue for Option A while shooting down Option B.

Your planning should involve thinking through—and jotting down on scrap paper—the points you think you'll want to make, in any order.

Let's consider the facts about Option A and how you could spin them positively. Or better yet, let's listen in on the student's (italicized) inner monologue as she re-reads "Option A"'s paragraph:

TIP

More Writing Samples fail for lack of planning than for any other reason.

WINNER: OPTION A

The first event is a free, self-guided walking tour of some of the neighborhood's private homes and historic buildings.

That will mean plenty of 1:1 conversations between homeowners and tourists—good for recruiting new members. "Free" lowers barriers to participation. And "self-guided" is great, will require fewer volunteer organizers.

The tour would feature the association's promotional table and exhibits of crafts, music, and cooking.

Showing off local skills and talents will make a good impression and involve town artisans. Leave leaflets about the association on the table.

Many neighborhood residents have expressed interest in such a tour.

Already wide awareness of, and demand for, this event means it'll be easier to publicize.

Some of the responsibility for organizing the event would be borne by those who own the homes and buildings; the association would be responsible for the remaining details.

If homeowners live up to their commitments, the duties can be divvied up so as to not strain association resources.

The costs of this event would consume most of the association's annual budget.

You have to spend $ to gain a big result. No plan is without risk.

Other neighborhood associations that have conducted similar tours report robust neighborhood participation and accompanying increases in membership.

That could offset the outflow of dollars. Are there dues? Dues would help. At least it's solid evidence that the idea has merit.

Sounds like the basis for a vigorous argument, but it's "argue for one over the other," so how might one demolish Option B?

> **LOSER: OPTION B**
>
> The second event is a 5 kilometer run through the neighborhood. The association has sponsored this yearly event for almost a decade.
>
> *Nothing new to get excited about. Those interested are probably already involved. Not much chance for people to meet and greet, get to know each other, talk membership.*
>
> In recent years, the association has hired a third-party company to manage the race and would do so again.
>
> *Ceding control could mean cost overruns.*
>
> Registration fees collected from race participants would cover administrative costs.
>
> *Breakeven doesn't sound so great.*
>
> In the past the event has led to modest increases in membership for the association.
>
> *Just "modest"? That doesn't sound like it'd fit the criterion.*
>
> At its peak, almost 1,000 people participated in the race, most of them from out of town.
>
> *Oh, great, bring in a lot of out-of-towners, none of whom will end up joining the association.*
>
> This year more people are expected to participate, because the course has been professionally certified and the race would serve as a qualifying race for a national championship.
>
> *Aha: Even less of a local focus than usual!*

Wow, she's rebutted every one of Option B's points. So it's all set, right? She should start writing, right?

We'd say, *wrong*. We'd say, "Be fair to yourself, and first think through the other side as well." A good advocate always marshals the arguments for the other side, so as to be prepared for all eventualities. And who knows? You might change your mind. So listen in as this very same student thinks through the assignment the other way around. Suppose she supports B, and works to weaken A?

BRAINSTORMING STEP #4:

Switch it up—figure out the arguments you'd make in support of Option B, while shooting down Option A.

WINNER: OPTION B

The second event is a 5 kilometer run through the neighborhood. The association has sponsored this yearly event for almost a decade.

> *There's already huge awareness about the event with which the association has been "branded." It's "their event" and can get a lot of hoopla. A real all-neighborhood event.*

In recent years, the association has hired a third-party company to manage the race and would do so again.

> *Awesome: This frees up the association's officers and members to work on recruitment and the year's other events.*

Registration fees collected from race participants would cover administrative costs.

> *Even better — the thing will pay for itself.*

In the past the event has led to modest increases in membership for the association.

> *So for years it's gotten more members in, routinely. If they really apply themselves to an all-out membership drive, the results could be amazing! Think of all the 1:1 conversations that can go on before, during, and after the race.*

At its peak, almost 1,000 people participated in the race, most of them from out of town.

> *Out-of-towners become residents when they like the new place they visit. A big push can be made to attract newcomers, who will have the association to thank for bringing the town to their attention.*

This year more people are expected to participate, because the course has been professionally certified and the race would serve as a qualifying race for a national championship.

> *Even more recruitment opportunities this year. And the national qualifying puts the town on the map, gives it visibility and credibility. It's a first-class event that will still leave plenty of money and energy to conduct the rest of the year's activities.*

Maybe you find this positive argument for B more effective than the one for A. Maybe not. But for your own sake, you're keeping an open mind, and acknowledging that each side has a good case to make. Moreover, we can poke a lot of holes into Option A if so inclined:

LOSER: OPTION A

The first event is a free, self-guided walking tour of some of the neighborhood's private homes and historic buildings.

> *"Free" could be perceived as routine; value-less. And self-guided means they're on their own, not thanking the association every step of the way. If the homeowners don't stay home to answer the doors, all you'll have are random people wandering the streets with no sales pitch for membership.*

The tour would feature the association's promotional table and exhibits of crafts, music, and cooking.

> *A table is easy to walk past on a walking tour, and the exhibits would have only a peripheral connection to living there.*

Many neighborhood residents have expressed interest in such a tour.

> *Talk is cheap; are they truly willing to participate? People can guide themselves through town with a brochure. How is that a big "event"?*

Some of the responsibility for organizing the event would be borne by those who own the homes and buildings; the association would be responsible for the remaining details.

> *Could get sticky, deciding who does what, and in the end the association will have to organize and pay for whatever the homeowners balk at.*

The costs of this event would consume most of the association's annual budget.

> *Throws the entire second criterion out the window.*

Other neighborhood associations that have conducted similar tours report robust neighborhood participation and accompanying increases in membership.

> *It's faulty logic to assume that what worked in other communities must be successful in this one. The association would be rolling the dice on one—kind of lame-sounding—event that would wipe out the rest of the year. That's way too big a risk to run!*

So which option should I choose?

That's easy: the one you think you'd have an easier time writing. The goal of the essay isn't to build membership in, and manage resources of, a neighborhood association. *It's to get you a step closer to law school.* And you'll have a more impressive piece of writing if you make the strongest possible argument for your case.

Look at it this way. You're going to be an attorney one day. Attorneys by definition have to be able to argue every side of a question. You could do a fine job defending either Option A or B, and the whole situation is fictional anyway, so don't sweat it. Pick the one you *want* to write—the one that'll be more fun, the one that'll show you off better.

At what point should I start writing?

We'd recommend the following rough allocation of time:

Study and deconstruct prompt—2 mins.
Brainstorm and plan—6 mins.
Writing—25 mins.
Quick last-minute proof—2 mins.

Should I just start writing?

No. Plan the whole essay out first, and pre-write your opening sentence. Once you start writing, you're committed; you can't erase or make changes without making a mess. Have the entire essay's flow in mind before you start to write.

Here's what our student—who has decided to make Option A the Winner—jotted down on her scratch paper as she brainstormed, and how she turned it into a plan:

1 Already wanted; much 1:1	1 Old hat; not too personal
~~Self-guided – little $ outlay~~	5 No excitement here
4 Recruiting leaflets/artisans	4 Cost overruns poss. w/ 3rd party
3 Known to work	3 Breakeven is NSG
2 Divide jobs to our advantage	2 Out-of-towners prob wont join
5 Take risks – charge dues	

Note that having jotted down her thoughts as they occurred to her—positive arguments for A on the left—she doesn't have to write out a formal outline. She simply numbers the points in order, and crosses out anything that doesn't seem to fit into what she has in mind.

All she needs to do now is try out a killer first sentence:

All indications are that the walking tour will better ensure reaching the association's goals.

Well done—especially in terms of using the comparative form "better" rather than "best." Her choice is clear, and people will want to read on to find out what the "indications" are and how she's interpreting them.

Wait a minute, that's "killer"? What about recapping the prompt first? What about an intro?

Naah, you don't need all that stuff. The prompt is right there for the reader to consult as he sees fit. Jump right in to announce your choice.

How should the essay be structured?

In ¶1 you will make the case for The Winner, starting with one of your stronger arguments.

Don't just cite a fact; explain how that fact is desirable, or leads to a desirable outcome, or helps to achieve the criterion.

Link your points with Keywords: "First of all"…"In addition"…"Furthermore"… "Finally."

Before ¶1 is through, acknowledge your Winner's weakness(es) and paper it/them over.

Open ¶2 by acknowledging The Loser's strengths, if any.

Go on to show why the negatives outweigh the positives.

Try to bring the essay back around to The Winner. And end.

That *does* sound pretty programmed.
Will every LSAT Writing Sample fit that model?

Yes, because it directly parallels the tasks as defined up front. You're making a case for one (in ¶1) over the other (in ¶2).

May I see an example?

I'll go you one better and show you two. For starters, here's an essay based on the earlier brainstorming of Option A, the walking tour, as "The Winner." The writer would of course not highlight the structural signals as you see below; we did that to make the point that judicious use of Keywords really shapes your essay along classical lines.

As you read, keep an eye on the assessment in the right-hand column.

TIP

Don't waste time recapping the prompt, which is there for the reader's reference if he wants it. Cut to the chase.

TIP

Readers love to see structural Keywords because their use indicates that you are an organized thinker and disciplined writer. Even for someone merely skimming the essay, such Keywords jump out and make a most favorable impression.

TIP

Save a couple of minutes at the end to do some quick proofreading for subject/verb agreement and tense consistency.

TIP

The more of these you write for practice, the easier they'll become.

All indications are that the walking tour will better ensure reaching the association's goals. **For one thing,** the neighborhood has already indicated that it wants such a tour, so demand doesn't seem to be in question. **Moreover,** the neighbors say that they'll handle their share of the organizing burdens, which suggests that it won't eat up either association funds or association volunteers. **Best of all,** the exact same event has been a proven membership builder in other communities. As members chat with nonmember residents, a pitch can be made to join the association. The promotional table will feature local artisans to make an even better impression, and leaflets could be placed there to encourage on-the-spot enrollment. **It's unfortunately true that** the walking tour would eat up much of the association's annual budget. **But** you have to risk some money in this world to gain a potential big return. **In any case,** perhaps the association can levy dues, or raise current dues, to rebuild the treasury so that other activities later in the year might still go on.

The run would certainly be prestigious and attract many participants. But it sounds rather impersonal; over its 10-year history it evidently hasn't had much of an impact on membership. And this year many of the runners will be out-of-towners attracted by the national qualification, unlikely to plant permanent roots in this neighborhood. The fees might cover costs, though "breakeven" isn't an especially dramatic goal to achieve. In any case, ceding control to a third party company might lead to cost overruns. It may not be wise to put the big membership push into someone else's hands. Having been around for 10 years, the run won't get people excited the way a walking tour would, an event we know the neighborhood already craves.

Gets off to a fast start, excellent.

"For one thing...so"; "Moreover... which suggests that" —excellent use of evidence–conclusion. Good qualified language: "doesn't seem"; "suggests that."

"Best of all" clearly indicates the #1 argument.

Acknowledge a weakness — yes!

Immediately brush it aside — yes!!

A clever, plausible possibility you've come up with; shows independent thinking.

Good: Grant the Loser its strengths.

Good solid reasoning based on evidence here.

"Unlikely...might...may not be wise" —all nicely qualified language.

Good conclusion, deftly turning it back to the Winner with no fuss.

In sum, that's a solid piece of work—unambitious, certainly, but you only get 35 minutes; you shouldn't be ambitious in the first place. Believe me, a solid, readable, well-organized essay is an eminently achievable goal in the time provided.

Did you see how little verbatim quoting the writer engages in? She doesn't say "The costs of this event would consume most of the association's annual budget"; she says "the walking tour would eat up much of the association's yearly funds." Not "exhibits of crafts, music, and cooking" but "the promotional table will feature local artisans." Putting some paraphrase spin on the details shows that you've thought things through—you aren't just parroting back words. It also makes the essay more enjoyable to read; that can't hurt.

I thought we were supposed to write a strong argument. How can all that qualified language—"might," "suggests," "unlikely" —lead to strength?

It's precisely *because* the language is qualified that the argument is so effective. Suppose the student wrote this sentence:

> *The neighbors will share the organizing burden, which definitely proves that the self-guided event won't eat up funds or take very many volunteers.*

No qualification there. But also *no room for exceptions,* and an argument with no room for exceptions is easy to weaken. You read this and say, "That's too strong! She can't be sure that money and volunteers won't be overused." Suddenly you are doubting her logic.

The original sentence is much easier to accept because it allows a modicum of wiggle room. It sounds less sure of itself, meaning it's more reasonable; that in turn actually means that it's *more* acceptable, on its face.

Now, just to prove it can be done, here's an essay raving about Option B and making out Option A to be fallible:

TIP

Bombast and overstatement don't make for a strong argument. Only carefully phrased conclusions, no stronger than the evidence justifies, lead to persuasiveness.

The 5K run is a real "all-neighborhood" event which already boasts the association's brand. It will pay for itself and be managed by a third party company, which will free up the association's officers and members to work on recruitment, as well as the year's other events. In addition, for a decade the run has been a proven membership builder. One can only imagine the amazing results if the association commits itself to a full-out recruitment drive. Think of all the 1:1 conversations about the neighborhood and association that will go on before, during, and after the race. True, the runners hail mostly from elsewhere, but out-of-towners become residents of a new place when they like where they're visiting. A big push can be made to attract this constituency.

The walking tour's success depends on too many variables, especially homeowners' willingness to stay home, answer their doorbells, welcome strangers in, and talk to them about joining the association. Otherwise you have people wandering streets with no recruiting going on. Furthermore, a promotional table is easy to ignore or walk past. Worst of all, this so-called event would eat up the entire annual budget, sticking a knife in any other planned activities for the foreseeable future. By contrast, the financially responsible 5K run is a first class, nationally significant event that will leave plenty of money and energy in place through year's end.

Wastes no time.

Lines up evidence emphatically.

Good structural keywords.

Concede a weakness and paper it over: Excellent.

Good value judgment based on evidence.

"Furthermore..." "Worst of all...": Excellent keywords.

As is "By contrast." Very good to get back to the winner at the very end.

Is one of these samples far superior to the other?

By no means. Either one would bring a smile to admissions officers' faces. Each is unambitious, well planned, well argued, and easy to read.

I notice that neither sample essay has any kind of separate, elaborate conclusion.

That's true. A conclusion paragraph isn't by any means necessary if you follow our "¶1 Winner / ¶2 Loser" format. Each of the samples segues gracefully from the debunking of the Loser back to the Winner and out.

TIP

Save one point or argument in the Winner's favor, for use in the final sentences.

What about proofreading?

Allot the final two minutes of the 35 for a quick look-see that attends to subject/verb agreement, dangling modifiers, unclear pronoun antecedent— anything that you can quickly and neatly fix with a carat (^) and insertion, or a simple cross-out and overwriting. Law schools understand that you have very little time to plan and write the thing; as long as what you write is legible, and doesn't look like a sea of cross-outs and scribbled insertions, they'll be fine with it.

TIP

Practice writing one or two of these a week! The more you practice, the easier it'll be to write a fine essay on demand…and the less likely it is that you'll even have to cross out or fix anything more than an odd word here or there.

I'm concerned about my LSAT score, and I don't want to take time away from the test to work on and practice writing because it doesn't affect my score. Why should I take the time to practice?

I am a good writer, and I had to write a few of these essays before I was able to crank out a first-class entry on any prompt, at any time. The LSAT Writing Sample is a very specialized task that requires some trial and error to gain expertise. However, if you need more persuasion to take the Writing Sample seriously, how about these arguments?

- **Students consistently report that planning and writing sample essays helps them with LSAT Logical Reasoning.** That should make sense. In creating a writing sample you are putting an argument together. In LR, you're taking arguments apart. Work on one task ought to inform your command of the other, and so students tell us.

- **Working on the LSAT writing sample offers a pleasant break from multiple-choice testing.** You can stop juggling (A) (B) (C) (D) (E) for a while without feeling guilty that you're goofing off.

TIP

The smart move is to do everything you can so that no single aspect of your application is anything less than first-rate.

- **Your stiffest competition is probably taking the essay very seriously indeed.** Those with high GPAs, great recommendations, and anticipated excellent LSAT results know that lots and lots of applicants boast the same numerical and qualitative credentials. As such, they look for any opportunity to stand out from the pack, and the LSAT writing sample is certainly one such opportunity.

Using the English language to make a case for one side in an argument should be right in your wheelhouse—if you truly have the mind and soul of an attorney. You should relish this chance to be a skillful debater and make the most of it.